W9-AQI-464

Jackie Robinson
and the Big Game

written by
Dan Gutman

illustrated by
Elaine Garvin

MCL FOR
NEPTUNE CITY
PUBLIC LIBRARY

Aladdin

New York   London   Toronto   Sydney

To my brother Jack
—E. G.

⊙✦

ALADDIN PAPERBACKS
An imprint of Simon & Schuster Children's Publishing Division
1230 Avenue of the Americas
New York, NY 10020
Text copyright © 2006 by Dan Gutman
Illustrations copyright © 2006 by Elaine Garvin
All rights reserved, including the right of
reproduction in whole or in part in any form.
READY-TO-READ is a registered trademark of Simon & Schuster, Inc.
ALADDIN PAPERBACKS, CHILDHOOD OF FAMOUS AMERICANS,
and colophon are trademarks of Simon & Schuster, Inc.
Designed by Lisa Vega
The text of this book was set in 18-Point Century Old Style.
Manufactured in the United States of America
First Aladdin Paperbacks edition January 2006
2 4 6 8 10 9 7 5 3 1

Library of Congress Cataloging-in-Publication Data
Gutman, Dan.
Jackie Robinson and the big game / by Dan Gutman; illustrated by Elaine Garvin.
p. cm.—(Ready-to-read childhood of famous Americans)
Summary: Presents the childhood of the man who would grow up to
be the first African American player in major league baseball.
ISBN 13: 978-0-689-86239-7—ISBN 10: 0-689-86239-3 (pbk.)
ISBN 13: 978-0-689-86240-3—ISBN 10: 0-689-86240-7 (library ed.)
1. Robinson, Jackie, 1919–1972—Childhood and youth—Juvenile literature.
2. Baseball players—United States—Biography—Juvenile literature.
[1. Robinson, Jackie, 1919–1972—Childhood and youth. 2. Baseball players.
3. African Americans—Biography.] I. Garvin, Elaine, ill. II. Title.
III. Series: Ready-to-read childhood of the famous Americans.
GV865.R6G88 2005
796.357'092—dc21

2002155969

Jackie Robinson
and the Big Game

Plick! Plock!

The little white ball

zipped back and forth.

PASADENA YOUTH TABLE
TENNIS TOURNAMENT.
TEN DOLLAR GRAND PRIZE.

"I bet I could win,"
nine-year-old Jackie Robinson
told his friends.

"Jackie, you never played
Ping-Pong in your life!"

"How hard could it be?"
Jackie asked.

Jackie watched carefully,

and learned very fast.

He beat everyone in the contest!

By the end of the morning

he had become

the best Ping-Pong player

in Pasadena, California.

Jackie ran home for lunch.
He gave the money he won
to his mother.

Jackie's brothers and sister
admired his trophy.
"Nice," his brother Mack said,
"but you can't run
as fast as me."

Jackie could never

turn down a dare.

But Mack was fourteen.

He was bigger and stronger.

He beat Jackie easily

every time.

After lunch

the kids on Pepper Street

played Chase the Fox.

They would link arms
and try to prevent
the kid in the middle
from running away.
Mack was the fastest fox.
Nobody could catch him.

"Let's see who can jump
   the farthest," Mack said
   as he and Jackie walked home.
"Let's see who can hit
   that tree with a rock."

No matter what game they played,
Mack always won.

Jackie didn't like to lose.
He ran home, stomped
upstairs, slammed his bedroom door,
and ripped Mack's shoes!

Jackie's mother was angry when she
saw the shoes. But she knew how
much her youngest son hated to lose.

"One day you will be as big as Mack," she told Jackie. "You will be better than him at something."

But Jackie didn't think he would ever beat Mack at anything.

"Hey, Jackie! Want to play?"
Mack and his friends were playing
baseball in the park.

"No thanks,"
Jackie said.
"I don't know how to play baseball."

"Come on!" one of the boys yelled.
"Grab a bat."

Jackie stepped up to the plate.

Mack threw him a pitch.

Jackie smashed the ball

right back at Mack.

At first base, Jackie
watched his brother carefully.
When Mack threw the next pitch,
Jackie ran.

He slid into second base
in a cloud of dust.
Safe!
On the next pitch
Jackie stole third base.

"Don't even THINK
  about stealing home on me,"
Mack yelled to his brother.

"Oh, I'm thinking about it,"
Jackie yelled back.
As soon as Mack
got ready to pitch, Jackie took
off from third base.

It was a race to the plate.

The catcher caught the ball.

Jackie slid in hard.

He knocked the ball

out of the catcher's mitt.

Safe again!

Soon it was too dark
to play anymore.
"You're pretty good at
baseball, Jackie,"
Mack said as they walked home.
"I thought you said
you didn't know how to play?

"How hard could it be?"
Jackie asked.

When he grew up, Jackie Robinson became the first African American in sixty years to play major league baseball. Mack Robinson won two Olympic medals. The friendly competition they had as children helped make both brothers into stars.

Here is a timeline of Jackie's life:

1914   Mack Robinson born in Cairo, Georgia

1919   Jackie Roosevelt Robinson born on January 31 in Cairo, Georgia

1936   Mack wins two medals in track and field at the Olympics in Berlin, Germany. He finishes second in the 200-meter sprint behind Jesse Owens

1939   Jackie is a football, baseball, and track star at UCLA

1941   The United States enters World War II. Jackie enlists in the U.S. Army

1947   Jackie plays his first game for the Brooklyn Dodgers. They win the National League pennant. Jackie is named Rookie of the Year

1949   Jackie wins the Most Valuable Player Award. The Dodgers win the pennant

1955   The Dodgers win the pennant again, and go on to win their first and only World Series

1956   The Dodgers win the pennant for the sixth time in Jackie's career. He retires from baseball and begins a career as a businessman and civil rights activist

1962   Jackie is inducted into National Baseball Hall of Fame

1972   Jackie dies on October 24